Ice Cream for You

Harley Chan

Contents

We like to eat ice cream.

Ice cream is sweet, smooth, and cold.

Do you know how ice cream is made?

Collecting Milk

The main ingredient in ice cream is milk.
Milk comes from cows. Milking machines collect
the milk from the cows. The machines pump
the milk into a tank. The tank keeps the milk cool
until it can be collected from the farm.

A large truck collects the milk from the farm. This refrigerated truck is called a tanker. The tanker keeps the milk cool on the way to the factory.

Making Ice Cream

At the factory, milk is mixed with sugar to make an ice cream mixture.

The mixture is quickly heated and cooled to kill any germs that are in the milk.

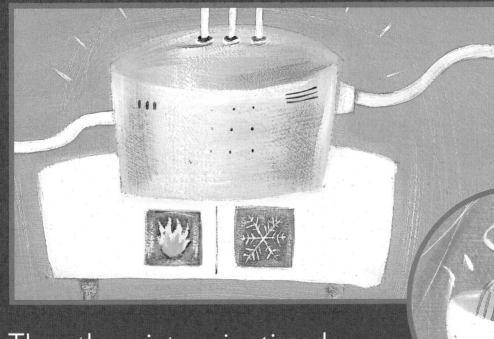

Then the mixture is stirred to get rid of lumps.

Flavors and colors are added.
Fruits, nuts, and candy can be added, too.

The ice cream is then put into tubs.
The tubs of ice cream are put into a freezer
to harden.

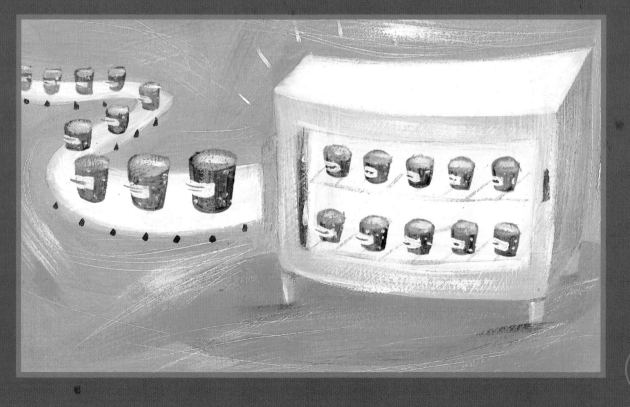

Selling Ice Cream

A refrigerated truck picks up the ice cream tubs from the factory. The truck takes the ice cream to the store. The tubs go into a freezer in the store.

You can choose from all the different flavors of ice cream in the freezer.

What's your favorite ice cream flavor?

Glossary

ice cream .... a sweet, smooth, cold food

milk .... a white liquid that comes from cows

milking machines ...... machines that collect milk from cows

tank .... a big container that keeps milk cold

tanker .... a refrigerated truck for carrying milk

tubs .... containers for storing ice cream

Index